Lemons and Lemonade

A Book About Supply and Demand

written by Nancy Loewen * illustrated by Brian Jensen

Thanks to our advisers for their expertise, research, and advice:

Dr. Joseph Santos
Associate Professor of Economics, Department of Economics
South Dakota State University

Susan Kesselring, M.A., Literacy Educator
Rosemount-Apple Valley-Eagan (Minnesota) School District

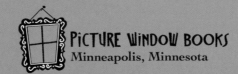

PICTURE WINDOW BOOKS
Minneapolis, Minnesota

Managing Editor: Catherine Neitge
Creative Director: Terri Foley
Art Director: Keith Griffin
Editors: Patricia Stockland, Christianne Jones
Designer: Nathan Gassman
Page Production: Picture Window Books
The illustrations in this book were
prepared digitally.

Picture Window Books
5115 Excelsior Boulevard
Suite 232
Minneapolis, MN 55416
877-845-8392
www.picturewindowbooks.com

**Library of Congress
Cataloging-in-Publication Data**
Loewen, Nancy, 1964-
Lemons and lemonade : a book about supply
and demand / written by Nancy Loewen ;
illustrated by Brian Jensen.
p. cm. — (Money matters)
Includes bibliographical references (p.   )
and index.
ISBN 1-4048-0956-2 (Hardcover)
1. Supply and demand—Juvenile literature.
2. Business—Juvenile literature. I. Jensen,
Brian. ill. II. Title. III. Money matters
(Minneapolis, Minn.)

HB801.L624 2004
338.5'21—dc22   2004019745

It was the third week of summer vacation, and Karly was bored, hot, and thirsty. Really thirsty. A tall glass of lemonade would really hit the spot.

"That's it!" she exclaimed. "I'll open a lemonade stand! I'll be rich!"

Soon, Karly was in business. She had a pitcher of lemonade, a cooler filled with ice, and a stack of plastic cups.

Karly's first customer was Mrs. Crane from next door. "Mmmmm, delicious, dear," she said.

6

Next came the boy who mowed Mr. Smith's lawn. He was so thirsty he bought two lemonades.

Josh and Shaun, brothers from across the street, sat with Karly for a while. Together they sold lemonade to a woman out for a jog, a couple of kids on bikes, and a babysitter pulling a toddler in a wagon.

Some businesses sell goods, such as food, tires, or clothing. Others sell services, such as cutting hair or fixing cars.

7

At suppertime, Karly ran into the house. "Look at all this money!" she said.

Mom smiled. "You did great. That money is called your gross profit."

"Gross?" said Karly. "I don't think so!"

"Gross just means total," Mom explained. "But remember, out of that money you still need to pay for the cost of the lemonade, cups, and ice. Those are your expenses."

"Well, I'll bet there will be some money left," Karly said.

"The money you have left is called your net profit," Mom said.

Gross and net are important business terms. Gross profit, minus expenses, equals net profit.

That night, Karly made a new sign.

"I see you've raised your price," Mom noted. "You're testing the market—seeing how much people are willing to pay."

"Exactly," said Karly. "I can't wait for tomorrow!"

The word "market" can mean different things. It can be a place where goods are bought and sold. But it can also refer to the people who make spending decisions.

Karly set up her lemonade stand early the next day. A garage sale was going on down the street, and people were everywhere. Business was fantastic! Karly was completely sold out by early afternoon.

"When people want what you're selling, that's called demand," Mom explained.

"Can we go to the store and buy lots more lemonade?" Karly begged. "I don't want to run out again tomorrow."

If demand for a product is high, and not enough of that product can be made, the result is scarcity. The product is hard to find and often expensive.

The next morning was cool and windy. The garage sale was over. Hardly anyone was around, and those who were didn't want cold lemonade.

Karly's Super Refreshing LEMONADE Just 50¢

"There's no demand today," Karly complained to Mom.

"Nope," Mom said. "It's tough to balance the supply of a product with the demand for it."

Karly nodded. She decided to close up shop. She wanted a break from the lemonade business.

In business, supply and demand are the two key factors in determining price.

15

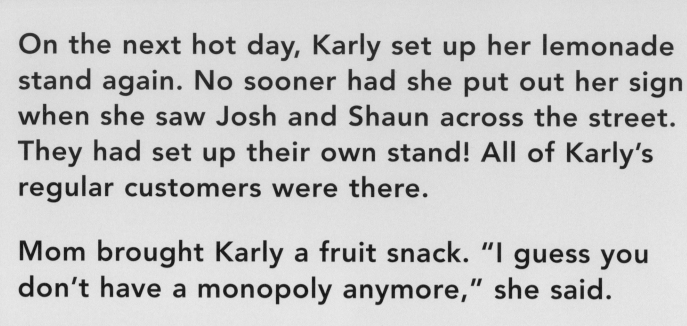

On the next hot day, Karly set up her lemonade stand again. No sooner had she put out her sign when she saw Josh and Shaun across the street. They had set up their own stand! All of Karly's regular customers were there.

Mom brought Karly a fruit snack. "I guess you don't have a monopoly anymore," she said.

"This isn't a game, Mom."

"I mean, your business isn't the only one anymore," Mom said. "You have competition. People have more choices."

Karly opened her fruit snack—and had a great idea.

"Be right back!" she said, as she ran into the house.

Karly returned with a bowl of fruit snacks and a new sign.

"You've cut your lemonade price to be more competitive. And by offering a new product, you've expanded your business. Nice going!" Mom said.

Fantastic Fruit Snacks 50¢

Now Just 25¢!

Karly's *Best Ever* LEMONADE

18

When businesses discount their products, they make less profit per item. But they hope to sell more of the product and make more money overall.

Business started picking up. Karly felt proud when she looked at the coins in her basket.

Later that afternoon, Karly was surprised to see Josh and Shaun walking toward her.

"We were wondering if you'd like to be business partners," Josh said.

"We have this friend who lives across the street from the park," Shaun added. "There's a softball game going on today. Maybe we could go there together."

Karly thought about all the thirsty, hungry people at the park. It would be fun to work with her friends, too.

"Great idea!" she exclaimed. "Let's do It. We'll be rich!"

How much did you make?

Sold 44 glasses at
$0.25 per glass

44 x 0.25 = $11.00

gross profit = $11.00

Supplies (capital)	Money Spent (expenses)
Lemonade	$3.50
50 plastic cups	$1.50
Ice	$1.00
Pitcher	free (borrowed Mom's)
	$6.00

total expenses = $6.00

Gross Profit		Total Expenses		
$11.00	—	$6.00	=	net profit of $5.00

Fun Facts

- In the 1600s, the Dutch used wampum—beads made of seashells—to trade with the Native Americans. Wampum was considered legal money until 1760.

- Every year, more than one million new businesses are started in the United States.

- There are 21.3 million businesses in the United States. Only 100,000 of these have more than 100 employees.

- The Gross Domestic Product (GDP) measures the total amount of goods and services produced in the United States in a year. The figure is put out four times a year and studied by economists. The number is so big that it's usually expressed only in terms of gains and losses.

Glossary

customer—a person who buys goods or services from a business

expanding—getting bigger

gross—the total amount of money a business makes, before subtracting costs

income—the money that is earned in a certain period of time

market—the people who buy things

monopoly—a business that has complete control of the market, with no competition

net profit—money left after expenses have been subtracted

partners—people who agree to be in business together, sharing the work and the profits

product—something that is made and sold

To Learn More

At the Library

Gibbs, Lynne. *Getting Down to Business: A First Guide.* Grand Rapids, Mich.: School Specialty Children's Publishing, 2003.

Giesecke, Ernestine. *Be Your Own Boss: Small Business.* Chicago: Heinemann Library, 2003.

On the Web

FactHound offers a safe, fun way to find Web sites related to this book. All of the sites on FactHound have been researched by our staff.

1. Visit *www.facthound.com*

2. Type in this special code: 1404809562

3. Click on the FETCH IT button.

Your trusty FactHound will fetch the best sites for you!

Look for all of the books in this series:

- Cash, Credit Cards, or Checks: A Book About Payment Methods

- Lemons and Lemonade: A Book About Supply and Demand

- Save, Spend, or Donate? A Book About Managing Money

- Ups and Downs: A Book About the Stock Market